LAW CAMP AS A RESOURCE TOOL FOR CHILDREN AND FAMILIES

(25 TOPICS FOR CHILDREN AND FAMILIES)

By: Veronica Brinson

Copyright © 2021 by Veronica Brinson
All rights reserved.

ABOUT VERONICA BRINSON

Veronica Brinson is a lawyer, author, aspiring wellness/self-development coach by training, and entrepreneur. She is also the mother of two adult sons.

In 2004, she started a law camp for youth in connection with her law office. The law camp was held yearly during summer months. It was held for one full day. At times, she would have additional sessions throughout the year.

She would invite speakers, politicians, and members of the community to share about law. She also would take the youth on various tours involving law institutions.

Here, she has made the details of the law camp into a book for families and children to use as a resource.

After graduating law school, Veronica Brinson worked for the federal government. Thereafter, she has held several positions in law including the operation of her own law firm for many years. She engages in civil, appellate, and criminal law.

CONTENTS

INTRODUCTION..1
1. BULLYING (Altez the Bully) 2
2. LEADERSHIP (Abby the Leader).....................4
3. MENTAL HEALTH EDUCATION
   (The Coach) 6
4. DEALING WITH AUTHORITY
   AND RESPECT 8
5. CONFLICT RESOLUTION (Mr. R,
   The Conflict Solver)...9
6. WHAT TO DO WHEN YOU ARE
   STOPPED BY A COP..10
7. PROPER ATTIRE FOR COURT 12
8. CAREERS IN LAW..13
9. STOP THE VIOLENCE
   (Daryl the Hater) 14
10. DRUGS AND MODERN-DAY YOUTH..........17
11. COURTS AND COURT OFFICERS..............18
12. MISDEMEANORS AND FELONIES..............19
13. PRISONS AND JAILS 20
14. WHAT IS LAW? WHO MAKES LAW? 21
15. THREE BRANCHES OF
    GOVERNMENT...23
16. LAWS AND HISTORY MAKERS...................24

17.	TYPES OF LAWYERS	25
18.	LAWS AND FAMILIES	26
19.	TRAITS OF A GOOD CITIZEN AND CIVIC ENGAGEMENT	27
20.	VOTING AND THE AGE TO VOTE	28
21.	PEER PRESSURE	29
22.	ADVOCACY	30
23.	HOW LAWS IMPACT MINORS	31
24.	GOOD AND BAD CHOICES: How Choices Impact You	32
25.	SCHOOLS/EDUCATION: For People Interested in Law	33
	SUMMARY AND CONCLUSION	34
	NOTES	36
	PHOTOS OF SELECT LAW CAMP PICTURES OVER THE YEARS	39
	LAW CAMP SUGGESTED ACTIVITIES	44

INTRODUCTION

WHAT IS LAW CAMP?

Law Camp presented by Veronica Brinson was started in 2004 as a way to introduce youth to the law.

The Law Camp was held in her law office. Thereafter, Law Camp presented by Veronica Brinson was held at various other locations too.

Law for many citizens is complex and complicated. A Law Camp helps the campers understand today's law and check out topics impacting us all.

Sometimes, we need a little more guidance about topics such as law and situations involving law to help us understand it better.

Let's do it from a law camp perspective.

It is a camp: Creating an atmosphere for law to manifest good purpose. Thus, sit back, relax, learn, and explore law.

1. BULLYING (Altez the Bully)

Bullying is so mean. It can give the victim a lot of fear. Children who bully become adults who bully.

Bullies like to use their power gained in social settings or systems to demean and humiliate others.

Some victims of bullies quit schools. Some victims of bullies quit their jobs. Some victims of bullies hurt themselves and others in an attempt to stop the bullying.

Some bullies get a lot of joy from hurting and humiliating others.

Bullies should not be tolerated in any setting.

How do we address bullying today? Bullies profit from the fear of its victims.

Bullies use various tactics to scare and intimidate their victims. Sadly, others may join in or condone it.

Bullies prey on folks different from them or vulnerable in some capacity. Bullies prey upon folks who appear alone. Bullies prey on those with fear.

One has to stand up to bullies or else bullies gets their power from the fear of others. Bullies feed off of the fear of those bullied.

Altez was a bully. His father was a bully. His grandfather was a bully. He learned bullying from watching his elders bully people. His elders, who would bully people, thought it was entertaining seeing others in fear of their bully tactics.

Altez liked to pick on people who were alone with little or no friends. He chose to pick on a little girl named

Vanessa. Vanessa often sat by herself and she walked home from school alone.

Altez would call her names and get her in trouble with the principal. He knew the principal's secretary and he would make up stuff to get Vanessa in trouble.

Because Vanessa did not have many friends, she did not have anyone to talk to about Altez's tactics.

Altez even started making Vanessa bring him money to school to not pick on her in front of others or not to make up stuff so the principal would not punish her.

Vanessa often wanted to just disappear. She dreaded coming to school.

One day when she was crying at home about not going to school, she revealed to her mom that all of her allowances had been paid to Altez so that he would not get her in trouble with the principal.

Vanessa's mother was a single parent. She did not have much money and she was upset to learn about Altez's bullying tactics.

Vanessa's mother told her not to ever give Altez's money again and to stand up to him. Vanessa stopped giving Altez her allowances.

She then told him in front of the cafeteria full room that she would not give him any more money and that she was not afraid of him.

Altez was embarrassed and he stopped bullying Vanessa.

2. LEADERSHIP (Abby the Leader)

The great debate has been whether leaders are born or made. Some leaders are born. Some leaders are made. Leaders serve others. Leaders stand up for others. Leaders know what must be done to complete the tasks at hand. Leaders lead.

Some say Abby was a natural born leader because she didn't wait for others to tell her what needed to be done, she did it when she saw the need. For example, at home, she would help her mom fold and organize clothes without her mom telling her to help.

However, Abby said she learned her leadership skills from her big sister. Abby watched her big sister growing up help her mother around the house, without being asked, and she started following her example. Good leadership leads by example.

Deandre won his seat for City Counsel of Mayberry. He was interviewed by an up and coming magazine about how he became a leader. Deandre shared that in sixth grade he ran for class president, and he won. He later shared that he was also in the leadership program in his high school. Deandre indicated that when he went to college, he again ran for class president of his freshman class and lost. He said in his senior year, he ran again for class president and won. Deandre says that for as long as he could remember, he has held leadership roles and he enjoys helping people pursue projects and goals in the community.

Often, leaders have learned their leadership traits from other leaders good or bad. Likewise, leadership comes natural for some. For others, leadership was observed, learned, and imitated. Leaders are elected officials. Leaders are non-elected officials. Leaders hold titles and some leaders do not. Dr. Martin Luther King, Jr. and many other leaders never held public office but lead people.

3. MENTAL HEALTH EDUCATION (The Coach)

We all know about physical education. However, people were not taught mental education in school. Mental health is a form of wellness.

We all strive for good mental health even in tough times.

Mental health is not about a person being "crazy." Mental health is something we all should value just like we do in our physical health.

Coach P which is what the coach at Northwest high school called him. Coach P taught physical education. He also coached football and other sports.

There was not a class formally known as "Mental Health Education." However, coach P would take 10 minutes at the start of his class every day and remind his student about mental health education.

He would say positive things at the start of a class like, "It is going to be a good day." He would make the class repeat it also.

He would make the class spend at least five minutes moving around in their places or stretching out before starting class.

Coach P would also play some positive and enriching music. Coach P would also say, "Hey, we got to work on our mental health education too."

How did coach P work on mental health education in his class?

(1) He started the day on a positive note.
(2) He included light exercises.
(3) He used music.

Mental health coping mechanisms are just as important as physical education. We have to learn how to cope with the meanness and stress in the world. Good coping mechanisms can go a long way.

4. DEALING WITH AUTHORITY AND RESPECT

Authority is defined as: "A person or organization having power or control in a particular.... sphere." (Online dictionary).

Authority, regardless if you like authority or not, we should give authority a degree of respect. Even when we disagree, there is a way to disagree without being disagreeable.

Authority can be parents, teachers, police officers, judges, or anyone in leadership roles presiding over you.

One must learn to effectively deal with authority, even when one does not want too.

You will always have someone over you or in charge pertaining to you. Parents are some of the first people with authority over you. Thereafter, we think of our teachers. However, in the employment world, there are people of authority. Police officers exude authority while monitoring neighborhoods.

Respecting authority does not mean that you allow the authority to wrong you. If so, there are ways to address such too.

How do we deal with authority?

(1) Disagree without being disagreeable.
(2) Show respect.
(3) Acknowledge the essence of the authority.

5. CONFLICT RESOLUTION
(Mr. R, The Conflict Solver)

We have to exist together in the world as civilized citizens. No man is an island. Therefore, in a world with a variety of different people, we will disagree on something.

I believe in fairness and seeing both sides of an issue. No one person is always right.

The girls in brown did not like the girls in purple. They would roll their eyes at each other daily. They could not work together. No work got done in class projects because the brown girls would not work with the girls in purple and vice versus.

They did not even know why they did not like each other.

Mr. R was the school counselor.

Mr. R then asked them to find something kind to say about the others. The two groups had so many kind things to say about each other from observation. However, they did not like each other and did not know why.

Mr. R told them to discuss the issue and if they could not find a reason for not liking one another to squash it and work together to make the school better. Mr. R said if there was a reason for not liking each other, solve the problem and work around the issue to look at the big picture.

The brown girls and purple girls got so much done thereafter at Northwest High School and collectively became known as the "purpbrown" girls.

6. WHAT TO DO WHEN YOU ARE STOPPED BY A COP

This is a sensitive topic these days. Be careful.

Share your thoughts on this topic.

What have others done when they have been stopped by a cop?

(1) Listen
(2) Be Respectful
(3) Try and remain calm

As I have stated earlier, listen, be respectful, and try to remain calm. There is no perfect answer. I encourage communities and families to continue to discuss proactive ways to address this matter.

Most citizens will encounter at least one stop by a police officer during his or her lifetime. Knowing how to interact with a cop may help the encounter.

I believe the best one can do is to try and not escalate the matter. It can be scary and dangerous under these circumstances.

In recent years, there have been a lot of publicity surrounding various incidents involving people and cops. Thus, this topic is so very important to communities everywhere.

I continue to think there should be a lot of training between civilians, communities, and the various police departments around the country pertaining to this topic. Candid discussions and solutions must be sought to create good community relations for all people.

An officer may ask you for your identification. If you have the ID on you, share it. I am a strong believer in being nice and respectful to all people regardless of race, age, nationality, disability, class, and more by both cops and community people. Likewise, regardless of any perceptions good or bad you may have of law enforcement, you should always: (1) Listen, (2) Be respectful, (3) Try to remain calm.

There are good and bad people in all professions. Whatever your experience is or has been, judge each situation on a case-by-case basis. I like to look for the good in people and organizations of all kinds.

Again, listen, be respectful, and try to remain calm. This is a very sensitive topic and in my opinion, it will require a village and community approach to start a conversation regarding this topic and to look at said topic from various perspectives. Share your experience and thoughts. Involve law enforcement in the conversation also.

7. PROPER ATTIRE FOR COURT

How do you dress if you have to go to court? Court is a formal environment. I suggest dressing up and at least dress business casual.

And some like to say, court is no "circus show."

One may even want to reach out to a lawyer or even a court staff to determine what is appropriate to wear to court.

It depends on the jurisdiction and environment.

Check out the attire of those in similar settings. Some wear a suit and tie to court. Some wear a polo shirt with nice casual pants or skirt. The proper attire for court depends on the particular court or courtroom environment. Courts are formal settings however.

8. CAREERS IN LAW

Not everyone wants to be a lawyer. However, there are various careers in law such as probation officers, police officers, judges, paralegals, legal secretaries, investigators, and more.

Probation Officer: Once a person has been sentenced, a probation officer works with the defendant (the person sentenced) and monitors his or her conduct on probation. Probation occurs in lieu of jail or prison.

Paralegal: A person who works with lawyers and assists with the preparation of legal documents and other legal matters.

Investigator: A person who investigates civil and criminal cases.

Legal Secretary: A secretary who works in a legal environment.

Judge: A legal officer who presides over cases and making rulings pertaining to people's lives, businesses, and other matters.

Lawyers: People who advocate on behalf of others. Lawyers may also serve in other capacities.

Police Officers: People who patrol the streets, investigate crime, and use arrest power.

9. STOP THE VIOLENCE
(Daryl the Hater)

Stop the violence and increase the love. There are a lot of violence and hate in communities today. People get mad about almost anything, then seek the wrong permanent solutions to real problem. When such happens, both sides lose.

Below is a poem depicting the sadness written by the author years ago:

In Memory of the Sons

Oh Lord, tears spilled from the lady's
eyes, as she cries over another son who
too early said "goodbye."

Mommy getting phone calls she
never wanted to receive.
Unknown voices describing bodies
deprived of what could be.

Mommy screams as her worst dream
come true.
A whole community should listen
because what happened to her,
could've happened to you.

Unripe souls going to an early cold
grave.
His life stolen by another brother.
Too late, neither brother was saved.
Funeral songs playing over and over
again.
Young boys leaving before they could
be men.

Women deprived of possible lovers.
Institution deprived of scholars.
Mothers deprived of sons.
Children deprived of fathers.
Our country without black men,
This is America's worst nightmare
and sin.

Oh, hear the screams of those mothers
who have lost their sons to an untimely
death.
Remember he who died at the hands of
a brother,
So that it may not happen to another.
Those of you who are now gone,
let your life be a symbol of what has
been wrong.

Together, we must solve this
catastrophe.
Her son is our sons.
What happens to her, happens to you
and me.

Think about what has occurred and the various messages and themes in the above poem.

Daryl the Hater

Daryl did not like Bo. Instead of talking to Bo about why he disliked him, Daryl decided to shoot Bo. Daryl shot Bo. Bo died. Bo had a family. Daryl has a family. Daryl was arrested. Daryl was found guilty of murder. Daryl will spend the rest of his life in prison away from his family. Bo is dead. Bo's family will never see him again.

Law Camp as a Resource Tool for Children and Families

Both persons and their families have lost due to the hate of Daryl.

Black on black killing is a big problem in the U.S. Violence is prevalent amongst other races too. How do we address the issue of violence? How do we increase the love and stop the violence?

Could Daryl have found love in his heart for Bo? Could Daryl have sought other ways to address his hate of Bo?

What are ways to increase the love in the community amongst fellow citizens? Some communities have used various ways to increase the love including sports, conflict resolution training, employment opportunities and community pride.

Work still exists to stop the violence and to increase the love and/or increase the solutions to hate and violence.

How do we change the mindset of hate and violence in our community? Perhaps, we should start very early in kindergarten classes and early grade schools addressing conflict resolution, collaboration, solutions and love over hate and violence.

10. DRUGS AND MODERN-DAY YOUTH

The "Say No to Drugs Campaign" started years ago but it is still a big problem. Good people are destroyed by drug use. Many families have loved ones who are plagued by drug addiction.

Drug addiction can stop folks with potential because it hinders their progress. People with drug addictions often acquire more problems because some do bad things to take care of their drug addictions. Drug addictions can lead to arrests. It can cost jobs and friends.

Drug addiction often occurs due to peer pressure and other societal ills. Continue to say no to drugs.

People who use drugs can seek drug treatment and other intervention options.

11. COURTS AND COURT OFFICERS

Courts are available for people to come and resolve conflict. Courts are governed by judges. There are others in the courtroom settings too such as courtrooms bailiffs, court reporters, and deputies.

When people have issues in real life, instead of taking the issue in his or her own hands, they can bring those issues before a judge in a court setting.

Some of the matters get resolved before lawyers go to the courtroom. If a matter cannot be resolved, a judge will set a date for resolution via hearing or trial.

There are various types of courts and in various states they may be named differently but generally are divided based on the subject matter.

I will use Georgia's court system:

* Superior Court handles felonies and civil cases.
* State Court handles misdemeanors and civil cases.
* Juvenile Court deals with matters pertaining to juveniles as well as other matters involving families.
* Probate Court deals with wills and other matters including family matters occur in this court.
* Magistrate Court deals with warrants, some criminal and civil issues with small monetary conflict.

12. MISDEMEANORS AND FELONIES

Misdemeanors are serious too but not as serious as felonies. Misdemeanors may be disorderly conduct, simple battery, and the like.

Misdemeanors carry about 12 months in jail if convicted. The sentence may also be served on probation.

Felonies can carry a life sentence. Some serious felonies are murder, aggravated assault, robbery, and the like.

Lulu was at a public party and she started yelling at everyone and throwing beer and drink cans on the floor. She was being very disruptive to the party and the police was called. Lulu was charged with disorderly conduct. Disorderly conduct is a misdemeanor.

Tim busted a window at a store and went inside. While inside, he took big screen TVs, high end watches, a lawn mower, and other items. He left the store but before he could go further, he was stopped and the police was called. Tim was charged with felony burglary.

The above stories are examples of a misdemeanor crime and a felony.

13. PRISONS AND JAILS

Jails are temporary incarceration places. People go to jails immediately after being arrested.

Prisons are long term incarceration places. People usually go to prison after being sentenced in a court.

Juvenile Detention Centers house the youth offenders.

Harold was arrested for drug possession. He was taken to the local jail. After the judge granted him a bond, he was released to go home. His charge is still pending but he can continue to work until his case is resolved.

Marlon was charged with aggravated assault. When he was first arrested, he was taken to the County jail. Later, he was granted a bond and released. Marlon wanted a jury trial. He was tried before a jury and found guilty. He was sentence to three years in prison. After his conviction of aggravated assault, Marlon was taken to prison where he will be for three years until his release.

14. WHAT IS LAW? WHO MAKES LAW?

Laws tell us what to do about a particular situation. Legislatures make laws. Legislatures are either senators or state representatives. Most legislatures are elected by the people There are also legislatures on the national level. These legislatures are known as United States Senators and Congressmen. (Even on the local levels, there are people who make laws such as County Commissioners and City Council persons).

What kinds of laws are there?

* Traffic Law
* Criminal Law
* Business Law
* Family Law
* Entertainment Law
* School Law
* Health Law
* Corporate Law
* Constitutional Law

Laws govern almost every aspect of society. We live in a civilized society. In order for people to get along and respect others' boundaries and properties, the laws exist.

Laws can be divided into civil and criminal law. Criminal law involves crimes. Most other laws are civil. Civil laws are those laws not criminal.

The Constitution:

What is the Constitution? There is a U.S. Constitution and generally the States in this Country have their own Constitutions. The Constitution gives us our legal foundation and constitutional rights. The Constitution of the United States is the Supreme Law of the land.

15. THREE BRANCHES OF GOVERNMENT

* Executive: The executive branch carries out the laws. This branch consists of leaders like the governor and president. Mayors are also considered part of the executive branch.
* The Executive branch carries out the wish of the land.
* Legislative: This branch makes laws of all kinds. These legislators are elected by their constituents. They are elected by people. They generally try and enact laws to support their constituents.
* Judicial: The judicial branch enforces the law. Laws set by the legislatures are enforced by judges and interpreted by judges. Judges do not make laws. However, the cases considered and ruled upon by judges may later make legislatures make, modify, or enact additional laws.

Various forms of government exist as discussed above on the state, local, and national level. Some of the forms of government are mayor, city council, county commissioner, school boards, sheriff, and related offices.

Johnny wanted to run for his state government. Johnny wanted to have an impact over every city and county in his state. Johnny wanted to be governor. This is an example of the Executive Branch of Government.

Dillon wanted to make and enact new laws to protect the elderly. This is an example of the Legislative Branch.

Tessie wanted to wear a robe and hold a gavel. Tessie wanted to make people accountable for the laws enacted. Tressie wants to be a judge. This is an example of the Judicial Branch of Government.

16. LAWS AND HISTORY MAKERS

Many history makers made history by changing and impacting the law. Let's talk about these history makers:
* George Washington
* Abraham Lincoln
* Barak Obama
* Shirley Chisholm
* Kamala Harris
* Harriet Tubman
* Dr. Martin Luther King, Jr.

These are just some of those who broke down barriers and/or became history makers.

* George Washington was the first President of the United States.
* Abraham Lincoln is known as the President who put forth the Emancipation Proclamation freeing the slaves.
* Barak Obama was the first black president of the United States of America.
* Kamal Harris is the first black and first woman to be Vice President of the United States.
* Shirley Chisholm was a U.S. Congress woman and the first black to run for President.
* Harriet Tubman is known for leading blacks to freedom via the underground railroad.
* Dr. Martin Luther King Jr. is the great civil rights leader who fought for civil rights.

There many other history makers of diverse nationalities and gender.

17. TYPES OF LAWYERS

Lawyers are prosecutors, defense attorneys, judges, insurance company lawyers, people lawyers, solo and small firms' lawyers, and big law firm lawyers, corporate lawyers, and more.

Lawyers generally go to school prior to becoming a lawyer. Lawyers go to school for approximately seven years. The study of law is a labor of love.

Lawyers can work in legal work environments and non-legal environments. Not all lawyers practice law. Some lawyers run companies. Some lawyers are politicians. Some lawyers run non-profit organizations.

Here is a look at various lawyers:

* Criminal Defense attorneys represent defendants accused of a crime.
* Prosecutors prosecute criminal defendants for breaking the law.
* Congressmen or Congresswomen serve the people in the United States Congress.
* Vice-Presidents runs the country along with the President.
* Former President of the United States such as President Barak Obama and Bill Clinton, they are lawyers. They also served as president.
* Many lawyers are commonly known for representing people as it relates to legal issues.

18. LAWS AND FAMILIES

Families use lawyers often also.

Families use lawyers in custody and adoption cases.

Families use lawyers to draft wills.

Families use lawyers in proactive ways and in other ways reactively if someone has gotten into trouble with the law.

Families use lawyers to consult about businesses and organize businesses.

Families use lawyers to represent someone charged with a crime.

Laws impact families in various ways. In many jurisdictions, there are family courts and juvenile courts which directly impact families.

All courts directly or indirectly impact families.

19. TRAITS OF A GOOD CITIZEN AND CIVIC ENGAGEMENT

* Kindness
* Respect
* Self Confidence
* Humility
* Responsibility
* Compassion
* Respecting other members of your community

Civic Engagement is how we engage in the community pertaining to issues of importance to us as citizens. Also, civic engagement is doing your part to help society as a whole.

What do you think are additional traits of good citizenship?

20. VOTING AND THE AGE TO VOTE

The voting age in the United States is eighteen years of age. Voting allows you to have some participation in the political process.

To vote, you go to polling locations. In modern times, people were allowed to vote via mail too.

In order to vote, you must register to vote. You have the opportunity to vote on political candidates running for public office. You have an opportunity to determine which political candidate has you or your community best interest as the platform.

Everyone has not always been given the opportunity to vote. Some minorities and women were not allowed to vote. Some people fought and advocated for minorities such as blacks and women to vote.

Tedria turned eighteen and she registered to vote. She did not know who to vote for in the election. However, Tedria longed to vote because she had read where her great, great, great grand mom was denied the voting privilege.

Tedria decided she would see which candidates cared about the issues in her community such as the violence and poverty.

Tedria begin to attend forums. She also checked the candidates' websites. Tedria also watched to see which candidate would reach out to her and her community.

Tedria chose to vote for the candidate who made decreasing crime due to violence a priority and the candidate which would provide economic growth to her community of mostly minorities.

21. PEER PRESSURE

What is peer pressure?

Peer pressure is the terminology assigned to young people trying to please their peers. However, even adults do so too. Good peer guidance is a good thing.

Peer pressure will cause people to hate other people because their peers hate other people. Peer pressure will cause people to use dangerous drugs because other people are using them.

Why do we have peer pressure?

People want to be liked and accepted of all ages; young and old.

Good peer guidance is good for some people. However, peers who lead people in the wrong direction can have a huge societal negative impact.

Jessica rarely bothered anybody. However, she wanted to be liked by the "in crowd." Beanie was the leader of the that crowd. Beanie bullied and terrified people with bully tactics.

So Beanie encouraged Jessica to go and spit on the new girl, Sandra. Everybody was harassing Sandra. So, Jessica said to fit in she should do it too.

The principal happened to see Jessica harassing Sandra. Jessica was suspended from school.

Peer pressure is when peers do bad things to fit in with their peers.

22. ADVOCACY

What is advocacy? Advocacy is when you fight for a position or a person. It is when you push for someone or an idea, issue, or agenda.

People use various tools to advocate:

* Letters: Some people write letters to the newspaper. Some people write letters to elected officials.
* Community involvement: some people join organizations regarding specific purposes such as the NAACP and other civic organizations with specific purposes.
* Running for Office: Some people advocate by becoming a politician and having a part in impacting laws.
* Protest: Protest has often been used to show disdain for something considered wrong.
* Courts: People use courts to resolve legal disputes using the assistance of judicial officers.

Topaz's best friend, Sopia, was the victim of bullying. She quit school because of her fear of a group of bullies. Sopia would not even leave the house because of school bullies. She once tried to even hurt herself to stop the bullying.

Topaz felt bad how Sopia was treated and started an organization called Friends Against Bullies. Topaz's organization would offer seminars and programs sharing stories of how bullies victimized people. Topaz allowed Sopia to speak at one of the meetings. The groups started raising money to hire peer pals to help victims of bullies.

The above is an example of advocacy by a person and a group. An advocate pushes for change or to implement ideas pertaining to issues of importance.

23. HOW LAWS IMPACT MINORS.

(A minor is a person under the age of eighteen.)

Examples of laws impacting minors:

* Laws govern the age one starts school.
* Laws govern the age of majority. In many states the age of majority is eighteen years of age.
* Laws govern when a person can officially discontinue his/her education.
* Laws govern the age one obtains his or her driver's license.
* Laws allow minors certain rights and inputs at a particular age.

Again, laws govern almost every aspect of one's life.

24. GOOD AND BAD CHOICES: How Choices Impact You.

We make choices in life. Every choice leads us in one direction or another. Some choices are good. Some choices are bad.

Think of the choices you have made in your life and how it has impacted you. Were the choices good? Or were the choices bad? These choices may also involve the wrong associations too. Wrong associations are those associations of any kind which cause you to get into trouble and act wrongfully.

Taylor decided that she would go to school each day. So, Taylor went to school each day. Taylor made good grades. Taylor was involved in sports and activities. Taylor finished high school. Taylor decided to join the military. Taylor made choices considered good by society. Taylor's choices directly and indirectly helped society too.

Tim decided that school was boring. He didn't seek help with his work. Tim decided it was better to quit school and hang out with his friends who also quit school. Tim started using drugs. One day while high on drugs, Tim was encouraged to rob a store. Someone saw Tim rob the store. The police picked Tim up. Tim went to prison for a long time. Tim's choices directly and indirectly impacted him and society in bad ways.

Both Taylor and Tim made choices and their choices, impacted their lives.

25. SCHOOLS/EDUCATION: For People Interested in Law

Lawyers usually attend college for four years and later a law school. Law school usually takes an additional three years.

Some people attend a four-year college to become a probation officer or a paralegal.

Some institutions have one and/or two-year programs for paralegals and other legal professionals.

SUMMARY AND CONCLUSION

Law Camp, the book, provides an opportunity to camp and explore law in a book format.

To summarize, law governs almost every aspect of our lives. Law is a career opportunity in many ways as shared above.

Law is a career opportunity. There are judges, lawyers, probation officers, police officers, and congressmen/congresswomen. You can also be a lawyer and not practice law.

There are several forms of government including local, state, and national levels. The President of the United States and other national officers preside at the national level. Governors and other state officers preside at the state level. Mayors and other local officers preside at the local level. One may receive a legal education via self-education, colleges, law school, and other educational institutions. Depending on the use of said education, a higher education degree is required in many instances. Some people in law attend technical schools and colleges for their education. Lawyers usually attend a four-year institution of learning such as college followed by attendance at a law school. People can acquire general knowledge about law also via self-study.

Law Camp, the book, teaches us even more about leadership, mental health education, bullying, law's impact, and much more. To reach Veronica Brinson, call or text 478-262-6770 or email here at attorneybrinson@gmail.com.

Veronica Brinson's mailing address is P.O. Box 174, Macon, Georgia 31202.

NOTES

NOTES

NOTES

NOTES

PHOTOS OF SELECT LAW CAMP PICTURES OVER THE YEARS

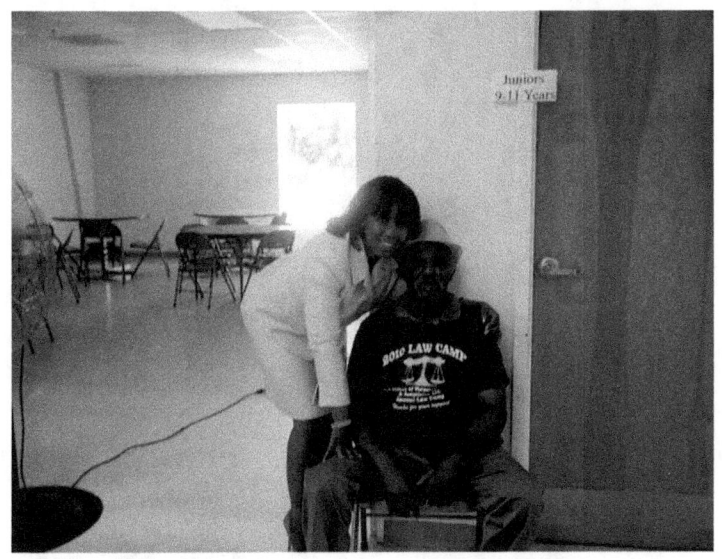

My father and I at a Law Camp with family.

Law Camp as a Resource Tool for Children and Families

My son and I at my law office. My son served as my paralegal.

At one time, both sons worked with me at my law office. There are many types of attorneys. I am an attorney in private practice operating my own business as an entrepreneur.

Law Camp as a Resource Tool for Children and Families

The poster at a former Annual Law Camps for families and youth. This represents the potential of our families and youth to soar like an eagle.

Veronica Brinson

LAW CAMP SUGGESTED ACTIVITIES

* Engage in family discussions about law.
* Get to know some law enforcement people.
* Visit courthouses and ask for tours for you or your group.
* Invite various speakers to talk about law including lawyers, judges, politicians, law educators, and others.
* Organize a civil rights symposium with diverse people, groups, organizations and companies.
* Write an article about an issue important to you. Publish it in a publication of your choice.
* Participate in mock trials and elections.
* Have a Law Day as a group activity.
* Read books about history makers in law.
* Watch documentaries about law and history makers in law.
* Spend a day at a law office whether it is a private law office or public law office such as a public defender's or district attorney's office.

www.ingramcontent.com/pod-product-compliance
Lightning Source LLC
Chambersburg PA
CBHW070858220526
45466CB00005B/2036